Contents

The island of Alcatraz is surrounded by the San Francisco Bay. The nearest land is a mile away. The prison opened in 1934. It closed in 1963. Only a few people ever escaped. But no one knows if they lived to tell about it.

Alcatraz

Prison for America's Most Wanted

C.J. Henderson

SCHOLASTIC INC.
New York Toronto London Auckland Sydney
Mexico City New Delhi Hong Kong Buenos Aires

Criminals on the Cover

Top row, left to right
B. Paul Coy, Louis Lepke Buchalter,
George "Machine Gun" Kelly
(AP/Wide World, Hulton Archive/Getty Images,
AP/Wide World)

Middle row, left to right
John Anglin, Al Capone, Frank Lee Morris
(All photos are © AP/Wide World)

Bottom row, left to right
Dutch Schultz, Fred Barker, Clarence Anglin
(Hulton Archive/Getty Images, AP/Wide World,
Hulton Archive/Getty Images)

The text in this edition has been revised from the original edition.

Copyright © 2005, 1999 by Scholastic Inc.
All rights reserved. Published by Scholastic Inc.
Printed in the U.S.A.

ISBN 0-439-66703-8

4   5   6   7   8   9   10   23   12 11 10 09 08 07 06

Introduction

It was the 1920s in America. **Criminals** ruled the streets. Many of them lived like kings. They paid the police to leave them alone. They killed police officers they could not **bribe**.

Even when really bad criminals were caught, nothing changed. They ruled from jail. They paid guards to give messages to their friends. If the guards said no, the criminals said they would kill the guards and their families.

The police didn't know what to do. How could they stop these murderers?

A man named Homer C. Cummings came up with an idea.

He would put the worst criminals on an island surrounded by sharks!

The island's name was Alcatraz.

The super-prison would keep the toughest prisoners locked up for good.

1 The Super-Prison

Homer C. Cummings had a tough job. He had to stop the criminals. He had to get them into jail. And he had to keep them away from other criminals.

Cummings needed a "super-prison for super-**prisoners**." There, the criminals wouldn't be able to talk to their men. They wouldn't be able to **threaten** guards' families. They would be put away once and for all.

Cummings picked Alcatraz. It was a big, rocky island in California's San Francisco Bay.

There was an old prison on the island already. The nearest land was over a mile away. The water around it was cold all year. The **current** was too strong for swimmers. And the water was full of sharks.

Cummings was given five years to build his prison. He hired a man named James Johnston to be the **warden**. Johnston and

There were eight gun towers around Alcatraz. Guards were in contact with the main control center of the prison.

Cummings worked together on the prison. They made the old buildings stronger. They replaced old iron bars with steel ones. Then they added new buildings.

Telephones and radios came next. That way the guards could talk to each other from any point on the island.

Eight tall guard towers were built around the prison. Each had huge searchlights.

Tear gas came next. If prisoners acted up, the gas sprayed down from the ceiling.

Then the gun boxes were built. They were steel boxes set high on the walls. Guards would sit inside the boxes. They pointed machine guns through small holes. And they kept watch 24 hours a day.

Next, electric gates and doors were added. Guards could lock any part of the jail just by pushing a button.

Metal **detectors** were placed all over. Prisoners would pass through them at least eight times a day.

An Alcatraz guard operates a metal detector. Every visitor had to pass through it on their way into the prison.

Barbed wire went on all the fences.

Cummings and Johnston then built one special room. It was called the control center. There was only one key to the control center. And all the weapons were kept there.

One man stayed in the control center. Dozens of microphones were placed around

9

This guard is working in the control center of the prison. He guarded all the guns, tear gas, and bullets.

the prison. This man could hear every sound in Alcatraz. He also knew if any phone was off the hook for 15 seconds. He could send a guard to find out if anything was wrong.

Guards counted the prisoners 12 times a day. They reported to the man in the control center. If anyone was missing, he called for help.

Johnston picked the guards at Alcatraz carefully. They were all **expert** shots. They were all good fighters. They were all tough.

There were a lot of them, too. There was one guard for every three prisoners. Most prisons had just one for every ten prisoners.

Guards stood in the towers and at every door. They watched the roads and the stairs.

The guards and their families lived on the island. Their kids even went to school there.

On August 18, 1934, Alcatraz was finished. Cummings and Johnston called it "The Rock."

It was time for The Rock to get some prisoners.

Why was it important to build a strong prison? What made it so tough?

Prisoners soon learned that Alcatraz was the toughest prison ever.

2 Prison Life

Reporters had lots of questions. Who were the first prisoners on Alcatraz going to be? Where were they coming from? When would they arrive? But no one was talking. Everything was top secret.

There was a reason Warden Johnston wasn't talking. Johnston was planning to put the prisoners on a secret train. And he didn't want the criminals' friends to find out.

He was afraid they would attack the train. Then the criminals would be set free before they made it to The Rock.

So Johnston kept the train a secret. At midnight on August 18, the train came to

Atlanta, Georgia. It stopped at a big prison. Guards made 53 prisoners leave the jail. Each had his legs and wrists chained. They moved onto the train. And when they were chained to their seats, the train pulled off.

The train reached San Francisco several days later. Even then, the prisoners did not get off. A special boat had been built. The boat had train tracks on it. The train was driven right onto the boat. The train was taken to the island.

More trains arrived. Soon, Alcatraz was full.

The prisoners quickly learned about life on Alcatraz. For the first few years, they couldn't speak to each other. They could ask for salt at a meal. They could ask for a tool at work. But that was it. Sometimes guards caught prisoners talking. Those prisoners ended up in the **cellar**.

Prisoners called the cellar the "Hole." It was a group of small cells under the prison.

Prisoners' cells are on the left. There were guards with guns behind the screens on the right.

Prisoners were chained to a brick wall. They stayed there 24 hours a day in the dark. There was no one else in sight. They were fed bread and water. Every 19 days they could have a shower. They could be in the Hole for ten days, a month, or even a year.

Every day on the Rock was the same. Prisoners got up at 6 A.M. They washed with cold water. They put on gray shirts and pants.

They marched to breakfast. There was plenty of food, and it was good. But prisoners who left food on their plates had to skip the next meal. The next time it happened, they were sent to the Hole for ten days.

The rest of the day was spent working and eating. On Sunday, prisoners got a two-hour break in the yard. They could go to church. But if they did, they got less time in the yard.

Day after day passed. Each one was the same. No one spoke. No radios played. Visitors were allowed only once a month.

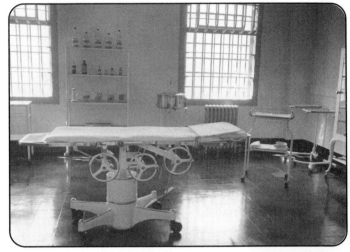

AP/Wide World

This is the prison hospital. See the bars on the windows? Even sick prisoners weren't trusted!

David Ryan/Photo 20-20/PNI

This is a prisoner's cell. Prisoners spent most of their time here. They were rarely allowed to talk. They couldn't listen to music.

And a guard was always there, listening.

This life drove some prisoners crazy. A prisoner named Al Loomis spent 16 months on Alcatraz. "It's driving the men nuts," Loomis said. "The walls were the barest things I ever saw. If a man tried to put up a photo of his mother, he was headed for the Hole. They never give a guy a break."

Warden Johnston thought his rules were working. "We have some tough customers," he said. "But we've torn them down to size. We've let them know that they're not as big as they thought."

What were Johnston's goals? Do you think he met these goals?

Alvin Karpis was Public Enemy #1.
Could Alcatraz keep him behind bars?

3 Old Creepy

Who were the criminals inside Alcatraz?

One of the Rock's biggest catches was Alvin "Old Creepy" Karpis.

Alvin started his life of crime by breaking into stores at night. He was ten years old.

As a teenager, he helped other criminals sell the things they stole.

Then he met Freddie Barker. Freddie took Karpis home to meet his mother. She liked the creepy-looking boy. So she gave him his nickname, "Old Creepy."

Karpis spent many years robbing and killing and kidnapping with the Barkers.

He also thought of a new crime. He'd rob

Here's Karpis after more than 26 years at Alcatraz.

One of Alcatraz's "super-prisoners" was "Old Creepy" Karpis. He was sent to Alcatraz in 1936.

trains. No one had robbed a train in America in years. The Federal Bureau of Investigation (FBI) was proud of that. Karpis wanted to make them mad.

He did. J. Edgar Hoover, the head of the FBI, *was* mad. He swore he'd catch Karpis. Old Creepy just laughed.

It seemed like Karpis would never be caught. He shot his way out of more than one police trap. He was Public Enemy #1.

Finally, the FBI found Karpis in New Orleans. Hoover flew there to arrest him. Agents surrounded Karpis's house. When he came out to his car, they jumped him.

Hoover ordered his men to handcuff Karpis. But the agents had forgotten their handcuffs. They used a necktie to tie him up. Old Creepy just laughed.

Karpis was put in jail for life. He said that he could escape from any prison. In 1936, he entered Alcatraz.

He never escaped.

Prisoner Robert Stroud learned all he could about birds.

4 The Birdman

Robert Stroud was a murderer. He was sent to a prison in Kansas for life.

One day Stroud found a nest of **sparrows** in the exercise yard. He took the baby birds to his cell. He gave them bits of bread. He took care of them.

Stroud became interested in birds. He read books on birds in the prison library.

He brought more birds into his cell. He fed them flies and bits of his own meals. He built cages for his birds. He used a broken razor blade and an old nail for tools.

Stroud studied birds for years. He even wrote two books on bird illnesses.

Robert Stroud became an expert on birds before he came to Alcatraz.

A scene from the movie, *Birdman of Alcatraz*. Stroud was actually not allowed to have birds at Alcatraz.

Stroud was moved to Alcatraz a few years after it opened. He wasn't allowed to have birds there. He became known as the "Birdman of Alcatraz" anyway.

Many people tried to get Stroud released because of his work with birds. But Robert Stroud died in prison. He was 76 years old. He spent 56 of those years behind bars.

More than 17 of them were on the Rock.

Capone was the most powerful criminal in the world. Could he be stopped?

5 Al Capone

The Rock's most famous prisoner was Al Capone. By the age of 26, Capone ruled Chicago's gang world. In fact, he was the most powerful criminal in the world.

Capone sold **illegal** alcohol to millions of people. Drinking alcohol was against the law in the 1920s. Capone's business made him very rich. He was making about $5 million a year.

Capone was a **violent** man. He ordered more than 1,000 murders. Capone ordered the deaths of policemen, **politicians**, and criminals. He killed anyone who got in his way. He murdered many of them himself.

Capone, after five years in Alcatraz.

Al Capone was one of the most powerful criminals in America. He was behind more than 1,000 murders.

He would kill his own men if they didn't obey him.

Capone ran Chicago. He paid the police and politicians to do what he said. Most of them obeyed him.

Once the mayor of Cicero, Illinois, did not obey Capone. Capone found the mayor on the steps of City Hall. He beat him up. Policemen just stood around. They acted like they hadn't seen anything.

Finally, the U.S. government came after Capone. They could not prove that he had murdered anyone. There was no one brave enough to tell on Capone.

So the government put Capone on trial for not paying his taxes. He was sent to prison for ten years.

Capone was sent to a prison in Georgia. There, he paid the guards to do special favors. They brought him good meals and his favorite cigars. He spent his days eating, smoking, and listening to the radio.

Then one night he was ordered out of his cell. Guards searched him. They chained him and pushed him onto a train. Several days later, Capone had a new home: Alcatraz.

Life was never the same for Capone. The silence drove him crazy. His first week there he tried to talk during a meal. He got ten days in the Hole.

When he got out of the Hole, he wanted to talk about it. He got another ten days.

A week after that, he tried to pay a guard to give him news. That got him 19 days.

Capone had no power in Alcatraz. He couldn't get special favors. He ate prison food. He had no cigars. There was no radio. He had to clean toilets.

In the end, Capone went crazy. He would not come out of his cell. He spent hours making his bed.

In 1940, Capone was freed. He died a few years later.

Alcatraz had destroyed him.

Why do you think Al Capone went crazy in Alcatraz?

Many people tried to escape from Alcatraz. But did anyone ever make it?

6 Escape!

Warden Johnston wanted to make it impossible to escape from Alcatraz. But that didn't stop some prisoners from trying.

Teddy Cole was a murderer and a kidnapper. He was sent to Alcatraz for 50 years. When he arrived, he said, "I don't think I'll like it here. I doubt I'll stay long."

He didn't. In December 1937, he teamed up with a bank robber named Ralph Roe.

They sawed the bars off a window. They kicked out two panes of glass. They dropped to the ground in a heavy fog. Then they smashed a lock on the fence gate. They jumped 20 feet off a cliff. Then they jumped another 30 feet into San Francisco Bay.

They were never seen again. But that doesn't mean they escaped. The water was freezing that day. The ocean's current was very strong. Most people think the two men were washed out to sea.

John and Clarence Anglin were brothers. They were both sent to Alcatraz. In 1962, John, Clarence, and their friend Frank Morris decided to escape.

They spent months digging holes in the back walls of their cells. When the prison first opened, its walls were in perfect shape. But after 25 years, the salt air had worn them down. Now they could be chipped away with a spoon!

The three men had planned their escape perfectly. They worked at night. They were very careful.

Guards counted the prisoners' heads

Frank Morris, John and Clarence Anglin (left to right).

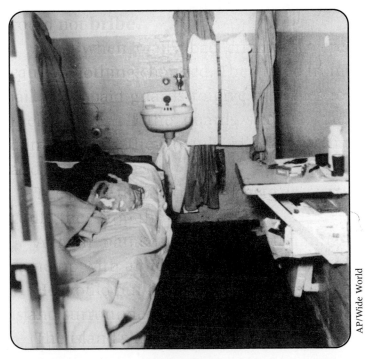

The three men above escaped in 1962. To fool the guards, they left fake heads in their beds.

during the night. So the prisoners saved newspaper, wire, paint, and their own hair. They made models of their heads. Then they put the fake heads in their beds at night. This fooled the guards.

Next, they replaced the metal air **grates** in their cells with fake grates. They made these out of cardboard. They hid their tools in an empty hall behind the walls.

By the summer, they had dug their way through the walls. Then they made their move. On the night of June 11, 1962, the three climbed into the hidden hallway. They climbed from floor to floor behind the cells.

They made their way to the roof. They walked on the roof to the north of the island. They jumped down and got into the water. They paddled away on a raft made out of raincoats. And, like Ralph Roe and Teddy Cole, they disappeared.

Did they make it? No one knows. No bodies were ever found. The current was slow that day. But the water was cold. And land was a mile and a half away.

These men had never been able to stay out of trouble. They had been criminals their whole lives. They were never arrested again. Do you think they made it?

No one will ever know for sure.

Which prisoners had the best chance to survive? Why?

For two terrifying days, the criminals took over. And the guards became prisoners.

7 **Riot!**

Most of the escape attempts at Alcatraz were very quiet. They ended without much violence. Then Bernie Coy tried to escape.

Coy was a bank robber from Kentucky. The guards didn't think he was dangerous. So they made him a janitor. He was allowed to go where other prisoners couldn't go.

It was Thursday, May 2, 1946. Coy was pushing a broom quietly around a cell block. A cell block is a group of cells. Coy's partner was also cleaning nearby.

Bert Burch, a guard, sat in the gun box above. Officer W.H. Miller was on duty in the cell block.

At 1:40 P.M., Burch walked into a walled-off section of the gun box. He couldn't see what was going on.

Coy knocked on the cell-block door. Miller came to the door. Coy hit him from behind. Coy's partner knocked him out. They locked him in a cell and took his keys.

Two prisoners lifted Coy to the gun box. He climbed to its roof and worked his way in. When Burch came back, Coy hit him with a club. Coy took a pistol and a rifle. Then he let the other prisoners go.

They all headed for the door to the prison yard. Coy planned to break into the yard. Then he and his friends would steal the prison boat. They would disappear into San Francisco.

But there was one problem. The key to the door of the yard was gone. Miller had taken it off his key ring. Coy and his friends could not get outside. They could not get to the boat.

They went back to the cell block. A **riot** began. And for 48 hours, the prisoners ruled The Rock.

Finally, U.S. Marines were sent in. They stormed the island and took over the prison.

Many prisoners were killed in the riot. Two guards died. Coy and two of his friends died. One of the prisoners was given 99 more years in prison. Two were killed in the gas chamber.

It was the only riot in the history of Alcatraz.

If the prisoners had gotten to the boat, do you think they would have been able to escape?

Today, people from all over the world come to see Alcatraz.

8 The Rock Today

Alcatraz was the most successful prison ever built. For years, the Rock kept the most dangerous prisoners in America locked away.

But in 1963, the Rock opened its doors. The prisoners were shipped to jails around the country. It cost too much to run Alcatraz. It cost twice as much as any other U.S. prison.

Alcatraz was an island. So supplies had to be brought over on boats. Even drinking water came in on a boat.

Frank Morris and the Anglin brothers had something to do with the closing, too.

Their escape shocked prison officials and the public. They had dug through the walls with a spoon.

The Rock was falling apart. It would cost too much to fix it.

On March 21, 1963, the Rock was shut down. Nine years later, Alcatraz became a park. Today, people from all over the world come to see it.

You can walk in and hear the doors close behind you. Then, when you want to leave, you can make your escape.

Why do you think people still like to visit Alcatraz?

Glossary

bribe *(verb)* to offer someone money to do a special favor for you

cellar *(noun)* a room below the ground

criminals *(noun)* people who do things that are against the law *(related word: crime)*

current *(noun)* the movement of water in a river or ocean

detectors *(noun)* machines used to find something, like metal or smoke

expert *(adjective)* being very good at something

grates *(noun)* grids of metal bars that cover something

illegal *(adjective)* against the law

politicians *(noun)* people who run for or hold a government office *(related word: politics)*

prisoners *(noun)* people who are locked up in prisons or jails

riot *(noun)* a noisy, dangerous protest

sparrows *(noun)* small birds with brown, gray, and white feathers

tear gas *(noun)* a gas that stings your eyes and makes it impossible to see

threaten *(verb)* to tell someone that harm will be done to them *(related word: threat)*

violent *(adjective)* dangerous; harmful *(related word: violence)*

warden *(noun)* the person who is in charge of a prison